Primary Sources in U.S. History

# The AMERICAN REVOLUTION

## Enzo George

Cavendish Square
New York

Published in 2015 by Cavendish Square Publishing, LLC
243 5th Avenue, Suite 136, New York, NY 10016

© 2015 Brown Bear Books Ltd

First edition

Website: cavendishsq.com

This publication represents the opinions and views of the author based on his or her personal experiences, knowledge, and research. The information in this book serves as a general guide only. The author and publisher have used their best efforts in preparing this book and disclaim liability rising directly or indirectly from the use and application of this book.

CPSIA compliance information: Batch #WW15CSQ.

All websites were available and accurate when this book was sent to press.

Library of Congress Cataloging-in-Publication Data

George, Enzo.
The American Revolution / by Enzo George.
p. cm. — (Primary sources in U.S. history)
Includes index.
ISBN 978-1-50260-250-3 (hardcover) ISBN 978-1-50260-249-7 (ebook)
1. United States — History — Revolution, 1775-1783 — Juvenile literature. I. George, Enzo. II. Title.
E208.G46 2015
973.3—d23

For Brown Bear Books Ltd:
Editorial Director: Lindsey Lowe
Managing Editor: Tim Cooke
Children's Publisher: Anne O'Daly
Design Manager: Keith Davis
Designer: Lynne Lennon
Picture Manager: Sophie Mortimer

Picture Credits:
T=Top, C=Center, B=Bottom, L=Left, R=Right

Front Cover : FC All images Library of Congress
All images © Library of Congress, except; 10, © Bettmann/Corbis; 30, © Shutterstock.

Brown Bear Books has made every attempt to contact the copyright holder.
If you have any information please contact licensing@brownbearbooks.co.uk.

We believe the extracts included in this book to be material in the  public domain.
Anyone having any further information should contact licensing@brownbearbooks.co.uk.

Manufactured in the United States of America

# CONTENTS

# INTRODUCTION

**Primary sources are the best way to get close to people from the past. They include the things people wrote in diaries, letters, or books; the paintings, drawings, maps, or cartoons they created; and even the buildings they constructed, the clothes they wore, or the possessions they owned. Such sources often reveal a lot about how people saw themselves and how they thought about their world.**

This book collects a range of primary sources from the American Revolution, from its causes to the outbreak of fighting in 1775, the course of the war, and the triumph of a new country forged on the battlefield: the United States of America.

The American Revolution began as a series of protests by colonial Americans against their British rulers, but developed into a fight for nationhood after the Declaration of Independence on July 4, 1776. The professional British army faced an ill-trained army commanded by George Washington. An American army thrust north into Canada failed, and the British gained victories around New York, but Washington's army recovered. At Saratoga in October 1777, it inflicted an almost unimaginable defeat on a major British army. The focus of the action shifted south, where the remaining British army was eventually pinned back at Yorktown, Virginia. The British surrendered in October 1781.

# HOW TO USE THIS BOOK

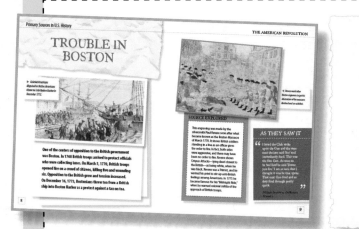

Each spread contains at least one primary source. Look out for "Source Explored" boxes that explain images from the revolutionary period and who made them and why. There are also "As They Saw It" boxes that contain quotes from people of the period.

Some boxes contain more detailed information about a particular aspect of a subject. The subjects are arranged in roughly chronological order. They focus on key events or people. There is a full timeline of the period at the back of the book.

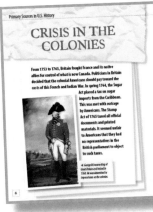

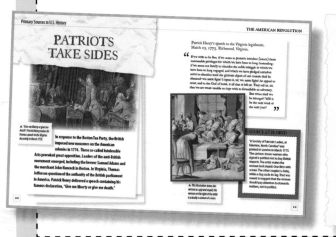

Some spreads feature a longer extract from a contemporary eyewitness. Look for the colored introduction that explains who the writer is and the origin of his or her account. These accounts are often accompanied by a related visual primary source.

# CRISIS IN THE COLONIES

From 1753 to 1763, Britain fought France and its Native allies for control of what is now Canada. Politicians in Britain decided that the colonial Americans should pay toward the costs of this French and Indian War. In spring 1764, the Sugar Act placed a tax on sugar imports from the Caribbean. This was met with outrage by Americans. The Stamp Act of 1765 taxed all official documents and printed materials. It seemed unfair to Americans that they had no representatives in the British parliament to object to such taxes.

◄ George III became king of Great Britain and Ireland in 1760. He was determined to impose taxes on the colonies.

## SOURCE EXPLORED

This is a proof sheet made to test the metal dies, or stamps, that the British government made to print the one-penny stamps that had to be attached to every piece of printed paper in the Thirteen Colonies. Each stamp has the number of its die written beneath it. The dies were carefully tested so they would be difficult to fake. Colonial Americans worried that the Stamp Act of March 1765 would lead to other taxes being imposed to raise money for the government in London. To make it worse, British stamp inspectors were allowed to search colonists' homes, shops, and stores. The colonists resented this invasion of their privacy.

## REPEAL OF THE STAMP ACT

In America, there were protests against the Stamp Act in many cities; many merchants boycotted trade with Britain. The British government came under pressure to cancel the act. Businessmen were worried about losing American trade. Many politicians questioned Britain's right to tax the colonies. In February 1766 the Stamp Act was repealed.

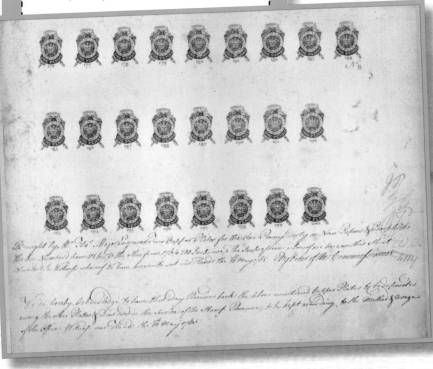

◀ A stamp showed that tax had been paid on a printed document. Newspapers and even playing cards had to carry stamps.

# TROUBLE IN BOSTON

> ▶ *Colonial Americans disguised as Native Americans throw tea into Boston Harbor in December 1773.*

One of the centers of opposition to the British government was Boston. In 1768 British troops arrived to protect officials who were collecting taxes. On March 5, 1770, British troops opened fire on a crowd of citizens, killing five and wounding six. Opposition to the British grew and tension increased. On December 16, 1773, Bostonians threw tea from a British ship into Boston Harbor as a protest against a tax on tea.

◀ *Revere raced other Boston engravers to get his illustration of the massacre finished and on sale first.*

## SOURCE EXPLORED

This engraving was made by the silversmith Paul Revere soon after what became known as the Boston Massacre of March 1770. It shows British soldiers standing in a line as an officer gives the order to fire. In fact, both sides were aggressive, and there may have been no order to fire. Revere shows Crispus Attucks—lying dead closest to the British—as being white, when he was black. Revere was a Patriot, and he wanted his print to stir up anti-British feelings among Americans. In 1775 he became famous for his "Midnight Ride," when he warned colonial militia of the approach of British troops.

## AS THEY SAW IT

❝ I heard the Club strike upon the Gun and the man next the lane said 'fire' and immediately fired. This was the first Gun. As soon as he had fired he said 'Damn you fire.' I am so sure that I thought it was he that spoke. That next Gun fired and so they fired through pretty quick. ❞

—William Sawyer on the Boston Massacre

# PATRIOTS TAKE SIDES

▲ *"Give me liberty or give me death": Patrick Henry makes his famous speech to the Virginia Assembly in March 1775.*

In response to the Boston Tea Party, the British imposed new measures on the American colonies in 1774. These so-called Intolerable Acts provoked great opposition. Leaders of the anti-British movement emerged, including the brewer Samuel Adams and the merchant John Hancock in Boston. In Virginia, Thomas Jefferson questioned the authority of the British parliament in America. Patrick Henry delivered a speech containing his famous declaration, "Give me liberty or give me death."

Patrick Henry's speech to the Virginia legislature, March 23, 1775, Richmond, Virginia.

> If we wish to be free; if we mean to preserve inviolate [intact] those inestimable privileges for which we have been so long contending; if we mean not basely to abandon the noble struggle in which we have been so long engaged, and which we have pledged ourselves never to abandon until the glorious object of our contest shall be obtained—we must fight! I repeat it, sir, we must fight! An appeal to arms, and to the God of hosts, is all that is left us. They tell us, sir, that we are weak—unable to cope with so formidable an adversary. But when shall we be stronger? Will it be the next week or the next year?

▲ This illustration shows the women as ugly and stupid; the woman on the right of the table is actually a cartoon of a man.

## SOURCE EXPLORED

"A Society of Patriotic Ladies, at Edenton, North Carolina" was printed in London in March 1775. The cartoon shows women who signed a petition not to buy British imports. The artist makes the women look stupid. One flirts with a man. The others neglect a baby, while a dog cocks its leg. That was meant to suggest that the women should pay attention to domestic matters, not to politics.

# THE FIRST SHOTS

The first shots of the American Revolution were fired on April 19, 1775. The British governor of Massachusetts, Thomas Gage, set out with 700 soldiers to seize Patriot weapons at Concord, west of Boston. Paul Revere rode to neighboring Lexington to raise the alarm. When the British reached Lexington, they exchanged fire with Patriot militia. In Concord, the British found the weapons gone. There was more fighting until the British retreated. They had lost 273 dead; the Patriots had lost 95 men.

▼ The Old North Bridge in Concord was a key site in the battle. This is a modern reconstruction of the original.

▼ The fight at Lexington was far smaller than this drawing suggests. The Patriots advance at left, with bayonets fixed.

## SOURCE EXPLORED

The French artist François Godefroy published this drawing of the Battle of Lexington in 1784. The French had supported the Americans against the British, and Godefroy shows the British soldiers in a bad light. He suggests that they fired cannons, abandoned their wounded colleagues, and set fire to buildings in Lexington. In reality, the fighting was a disorganized skirmish and involved much smaller numbers than Godefroy shows.

Pastor Jonas Clark witnessed the arrival of the British "Redcoats" [soldiers] in Lexington early on April 19, 1775. According to his account, the British fired first.

❝ Capt. Parker, who commanded the militia company, ordered the men to disperse and take care of themselves, and not to fire. Upon this, our men dispersed—but many of them not so speedily as they might have done, not having the most distant idea of such brutal barbarity and more than savage cruelty from the troops of a British king, as they immediately experienced! For, no sooner did they come in sight of our company, but one of them, supposed to be an officer of rank, was heard to say to the troops, 'Damn them! We will have them!' Upon which the troops shouted aloud, huzza'd, and rushed furiously towards our men. ❞

# BATTLE OF BUNKER HILL

▶ British Redcoats advance up Breed's Hill in disciplined ranks in this painting of the battle from the early twentieth century.

From Concord, the British retreated to Boston. They were followed by Patriot militia, who set up camps and began a siege of the city. On June 17, 1775, 1,200 Patriots took control of Breed's Hill, across the Charles River. Some 2,200 British troops sailed across the river and launched an attack up the hill. The Patriots let them get near the top, then fired. The British attacked again and were again shot down. At the third assault, the Americans ran out of ammunition and retreated.

## SOURCE EXPLORED

This contemporary drawing shows the battle on Breed's Hill. The American commander, Israel Putnam, had been sent to seize Bunker Hill, but dug his men in on top of neighboring Breed's Hill in error. The Patriot line is on the left of the picture. The British Redcoats advance toward the enemy, while British ships shell the American positions from the river. A British cannon is in the foreground. At the bottom of the hill, smoke rises from the burning town of Charleston. Although the British won the battle, they lost 1,000 men; the Americans lost about 400. But the British had learned that the Americans were able to fight a pitched battle. The Americans had learned that they could stand up to the feared British regulars.

## AS THEY SAW IT

" On Saturday last, the 17th, the Regulars attacked us upon one of the Charlestown Hills, where we had begun to entrench, & obliged us to retreat, by means of their Ships & Floating Batterys, we having no large Cannon to match theirs; the Cannon we cou'd have had, if we had had Gunpowder enough to Spare. "

—Joseph Palmer describes the battle in a letter to John Adams on June 19, 1775.

◀ The scale on this drawing is wrong, but it gives a clear impression of the positions of the enemy forces during the battle.

# THE SIEGE OF BOSTON

The Siege of Boston lasted for eleven months. In May 1775, the Patriots seized Fort Ticonderoga in upstate New York. That winter, the Patriot officer Henry Knox dragged the fort's sixty cannons 300 miles to Boston. George Washington, now the commander of the Continental Army, set the cannons up overlooking the city and began a bombardment. The British began to evacuate Boston on March 17, 1776.

▼ *This etching from the 1770s shows Boston as a typical European port, with British ships at anchor and soldiers on shore.*

In May 1775, John Andrews, a merchant in Boston, writes to his sister's husband about the difficulty of leaving town.

" You'll observe by this, that I am yet in Boston, & here like to remain— three of us charterd a vessell a fortnight since to convey us to Halifax as Sam dont think your city Safe by any means, but the absolute refusal of the Governor to Suffer any merchandize to be carried out the town, had determd me to Stay & take care of my effects, together wth the perswasion of Saml & his wife & Ruthy—the latter being perfectly willing & desirous of going without me, as her peace of mind depends entirely upon his leaving the town; in concequence of which have acquiesed [agreed], but am affraid it will be a long time before I Shall See her again, if ever. Near half the inhabitants have left the town already, & another quarter, at least, have been waiting for a week past with earnest expectation of geting Passes. "

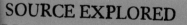

▲ *Revere's drawing includes recognizable Boston landmarks but emphasizes the number of enemy ships in the harbor.*

## SOURCE EXPLORED

Paul Revere produced this print during the tense years before the Revolution. It shows British ships landing troops in Boston in 1768. Revere published the image in 1770. The British warships look very large and powerful compared with the city. As a Patriot, Revere wanted to arouse outrage among his fellow Bostonians. The city was essentially under British military rule until March 1776, when the British left.

# AN AMERICAN LEADER

In response to the outbreak of fighting in Massachusetts, the Second Continental Congress had met in Philadelphia in May 1775. Delegates from twelve of the thirteen colonies—Georgia sent delegates later—elected John Hancock as president. Congress voted to create a Continental Army out of the Patriot militia camped around Boston. To command the army, they selected a Virginia congressman who had been a hero in the British Army during the French and Indian War: George Washington.

◀ *This engraving from 1781 shows George Washington in his uniform as commander in chief of the Continental Army.*

▲ The commission spelled out that the purpose of the Continental Army was "the defense of American liberty."

## SOURCE EXPLORED

On June 15, 1775, the delegates at the Continental Congress unanimously chose George Washington to be the commander in chief of the Continental Army. Washington accepted the post on the grounds that he would receive no pay apart from his expenses.

On June 17 the Continental Congress drafted this commission, which was approved two days later. It was one of the first official documents issued by an American Congress. It reads "To GEORGE WASHINGTON, Esq., We, reposing special trust and confidence in your patriotism, valour, conduct, and fidelity, DO, by these presents, constitute and appoint you to be GENERAL AND COMMANDER IN CHIEF of the army of the United Colonies."

## AS THEY SAW IT

66 The whole army raised for the defense of the American Cause shall be put under my care... You may believe me my dear Patsy, when I assure you in the most solemn manner, that, so far from seeking this appointment, I have used every endeavor in my power to avoid it. 99

—George Washington writes to his wife Martha on June 18, 1775.

# WASHINGTON'S ARMY

One of George Washington's most urgent tasks was to turn the volunteers of the Continental Army into a disciplined, organized force that could take on the feared British regulars. Many men joined the army because they were promised land at the end of the war. To begin with, there were no uniforms. Every soldier was issued with a water bottle, musket, helmet, bullet bag, gunpowder horn, and knife. Their supplies came from Britain's old enemies: France, Spain, and the Netherlands.

► *This print shows Continental Army uniforms from later in the war, after the American forces had become better organized.*

## SOURCE EXPLORED

This poster is thought to have been used to recruit men for the Continental Army during the Revolution. (Some historians believe it was actually produced in 1798, when an attack by France was feared—but that it drew on the spirit of the Revolution.) It shows poses from infantry drill. As many as 250,000 men served during the Revolution. To Washington's irritation, wives often followed their husbands; they did jobs such as laundry and nursing.

## THE BRITISH ARMY

The enemy facing the Continental Army was one of the best fighting forces in the world. The British Army had about 36,000 soldiers in 1775. They were well trained and experienced in colonial warfare, but they were spread around the globe. The British recruited more soldiers and hired 30,000 German mercenaries, known as Hessians. By 1779 they had a total of 60,000 troops in North America.

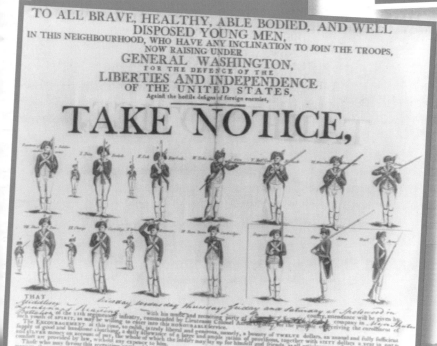

◀ Although this poster is often associated with the Revolution, modern scholars have cast doubt on the link.

# LOYALISTS

About 15 to 20 percent of Americans—around half a million people—remained loyal to the British. These Loyalists tended to be farmers, landowners, royal office holders and professionals, including the clergy. Some colonies had high numbers of Loyalists, including Georgia and the Carolinas; in New York, half the population supported the British. However, the British found it difficult to raise Loyalist troops for their armies as they hoped. Many Americans tried to stay neutral until it became clear who would win the war. When the war ended, at least 80,000 Loyalist Americans went into exile, many to Canada.

◀ This British cartoon from 1775 shows a Loyalist in Virginia being forced to sign a document by a gang of Patriots.

## SOURCE EXPLORED

This engraving was made in 1775 and published in London. It is entitled "The Patriotic Barber of New York, or the Captain in the Suds." It shows a barber in New York throwing a customer out of his store on learning that he is a British naval officer. The officer is half shaved and has not put his wig back on. The cartoon was based on a real incident.

▶ *The barber still holds a razor in his hand— this gives the image a threatening feeling.*

Major Walter Dulany, of the Maryland Loyalists, writes to his British commander to explain his divided loyalties after the Declaration of Independence in 1776.

“ My duty as a subject, the happiness which America enjoyed under the British Government, and the miseries to which she would be reduced by an independancy, were the motives that induced me to join the British Army; nor are there any dangers, or difficulties, that I would not cheerfully undergo, to effect a happy restoration.

But, at the same time, that I acted, with the greatest zeal, against my rebellious countrymen, I never forgot that I was an American. If therefore, sir, Independence should be granted, and the war still continued, I should deem it extremely improper to remain in a situation, obliging me to act either directly or indirectly against America. ”

# THE WAR IN CANADA

With the capture of Fort Ticonderoga in New York in May 1775, the way to Canada was open. General Richard Montgomery led a Patriot army north. The Americans soon captured Montreal, but at the start of an attack on the fortress of Quebec on December 31, 1775, Montgomery was killed. The attack ended in a total defeat for the Americans, who withdrew. The British retained control of Canada throughout the rest of the Revolution.

▼ *This view of the fortress and city of Quebec was drawn by a French naval officer in 1768. The city's defenses proved too strong for the Patriot attack.*

◀ *When this portrait was created, it was fashionable to portray people as being much taller than they actually were.*

## SOURCE EXPLORED

This engraving of General Richard Montgomery was published in 1777, two years after his death at Quebec. It shows the soldier in his uniform. His pose looks unnatural: he is leaning on his elbow on a bank. The image is based on heroic poses from classical statues, which makes Montgomery appear tall and slim, like an athletic young man.

Captain Aaron Burr was with Montgomery as he led the attack on Quebec during a snowstorm. He later wrote this report of how the Americans cut through a barricade.

❝ The first barrier to be surmounted was at the Pot-Ash. In front of it was a blockhouse and picket, in charge of some Canadians, who, after making a single fire, fled in confusion. On advancing to force the barrier, an accidental discharge of a piece of artillery from the British battery, when the American front was in forty paces of it, killed General Montgomery, Captain McPherson, one of his aids, Captain Cheeseman, and every other person in front, except Captain Burr and a French guide. ❞

# DECLARATION OF INDEPENDENCE

▲ *The room where Congress adopted the Declaration of Independence has been re-created in Philadelphia.*

In June 1776 the Second Continental Congress selected a committee, headed by Thomas Jefferson, to draft a declaration of independence. After making eighty changes to his original draft, Congress adopted the declaration on July 4, 1776. The British rejected the American right to claim independence. In American eyes, the Revolutionary War was no longer a civil war but a war between two sovereign nations.

◀ The facsimile created by William Stone is the most famous version of the document.

◀ *The facsimile created by William Stone is the most famous version of the document.*

## THE SIGNERS

A total of 56 delegates at the Continental Congress signed the Declaration of Independence. In the middle of the top row of signatures is that of John Hancock, the president of the Congress. Although it is widely believed that the declaration was signed on July 4, 1776, it might have been up to a month later that all the signatures were completed.

## SOURCE EXPLORED

This is a facsimile of the Declaration of Independence. When the original began to fade, in 1823 Secretary of State John Quincy Adams asked the engraver William Stone to make a copy. The work took Stone three years. No one knows how he copied the original document—complete with the signatures—so accurately. He may have traced it and engraved it into a sheet of copper. He may have damped the ink on the original document so that he could press another sheet of paper on top of it to take a copy. When Stone had finished, he made 200 copies of the Declaration. They were given to official bodies and to the original signers who survived, such as Thomas Jefferson and John Adams.

# BATTLES FOR NEW YORK

After a series of defeats in late 1776, Washington's Continental Army was in New Jersey. New York remained a British stronghold. On Christmas Night, Washington launched a surprise attack across the Delaware River. The Americans won a victory in the Battle of Trenton, which set up another at Princeton, New Jersey, in January 1777.

▼ *This painting of Washington crossing the Delaware is not very realistic—no one would stand up in a boat on a dangerous river crossing.*

Elisha Bostwick was a private in the Continental Army.
He recalls crossing the Delaware with Washington.

" [O]ur whole army was then set on motion and toward evening
began to re-cross the Delaware but by obstructions of ice in the river
did not all get across till quite late in the evening, and all the time a
constant fall of snow with some rain, and finally our march began
with the torches of our field pieces stuck in the exhalters [smoke
holes]. [They] sparkled and blazed in the storm all night and about
daylight a halt was made at which time his Excellency (General
Washington) and aides came near to the front on the side of the path
where the soldiers stood. "

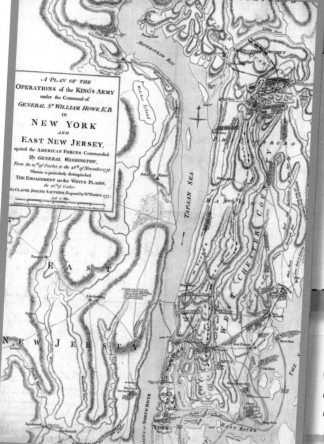

## SOURCE EXPLORED

This map of New York and New
Jersey was drawn in 1777 by
Claude Joseph Sauthier for the
British government. It shows the
movements of British and American
troops in the area in October and
November 1776. The British won a
victory at the Battle of White Plains
on October 28. It helped drive
Washington away from New York
and strengthen the British position.

◄ Having good maps
was essential for military
commanders, so both sides
employed good mapmakers.

# BATTLE OF SARATOGA

The British planned to isolate New England by a pincer movement south from Canada and north from New York. By August 1777, however, the British faced supply shortages. In clashes in the early fall, they were heavily outnumbered by the Americans. With no reinforcements arriving, General John Burgoyne surrendered at Saratoga on October 17, 1777. It was the turning point of the war.

▼ *Authentic cannon still stand on the battlefield at Saratoga, which is now a National Historical Park.*

▲ This engraving shows the dismay of the British as they surrender. It was one of the most shocking defeats in British military history.

## SOURCE EXPLORED

A British officer turns away as General John Burgoyne surrenders to American general Horatio Gates at the Battle of Saratoga on October 17, 1777. This engraving was made soon after the event. It shows Burgoyne giving Gates his sword as a sign of surrender. In reality, Gates returned it to his enemy as a mark of respect. The artist shows how shocking the defeat was for the British. Burgoyne is covered in dark shadow. On the right an American drummer boy plays. While the 6,000 British troops gave up their arms, American musicians played "Yankee Doodle." The song had been written in Britain to poke fun at the Americans, but the Patriots adopted it as an anthem.

## DECISIVE BATTLE

The British defeat at Saratoga changed the war. It showed that the Americans had real hopes of victory, which encouraged the French to side with them. French supplies of arms, money, and ships were a huge benefit to the American cause. For the British, it was shocking to realize that the regular army could be defeated by a colonial force.

# WINTER AT VALLEY FORGE

▲ In this later painting, Washington is moved by the dedication of his men during the cold winter at Valley Forge.

Washington's exhausted army spent the winter of 1777 at Valley Forge, Pennsylvania. The 12,000 soldiers faced terrible conditions. There was barely any food. Many men fell sick, and about 2,000 died from diseases such as typhoid. But Washington and his Prussian advisor, Baron von Steuben, drilled their troops constantly. When the army left Valley Forge in spring 1778, it was a far better fighting force than when it had arrived.

◀ *The National Historical Park at Valley Forge contains original and re-created log cabins built by the American soldiers.*

## SOURCE EXPLORED

This log cabin stands at Valley Forge. Soldiers built the huts themselves so they did not have to sleep in tents. The huts were damp and crowded but gave some protection from the cold. Most American soldiers lacked proper clothing for a Pennsylvania winter: only one in three even had any shoes to wear.

Albigence Waldo was an army surgeon. In his journal he records life at Valley Forge.

" December 21–(Valley Forge) Preparations made for huts. Provisions Scarce. Mr Ellis went homeward–sent a Letter to my Wife. Heartily wish myself at home, my Skin & eyes are almost spoil'd with continual smoke. A general cry thro' the Camp this Evening among the Soldiers, 'No Meat! No Meat!'–the Distant vales Echoed back the melancholy sound–'No Meat! No Meat!'... What have you for your Dinner Boys? 'Nothing but Fire Cake and Water, Sir.' At night, 'Gentlemen the Supper is ready.' What is your Supper Lads? 'Fire Cake and Water, Sir.' Very poor beef has been drawn in our Camp the greater part of this season. "

# CHANGING FORTUNES

After the defeat at Saratoga, the focus turned south. In South Carolina, the British used Loyalists to pacify local Patriots. On March 29, 1780, they began a siege of the key port of Charleston. Within two weeks the city was cut off. On May 12, 1780, the Americans surrendered. It was the worst American defeat of the Revolution, and was soon followed by another defeat in the Battle of Camden. The American situation in the South was critical.

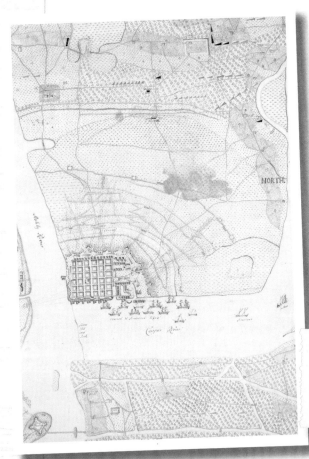

◄ This map of the siege lines in Charleston was drawn by a British officer soon after the siege ended in May 1780.

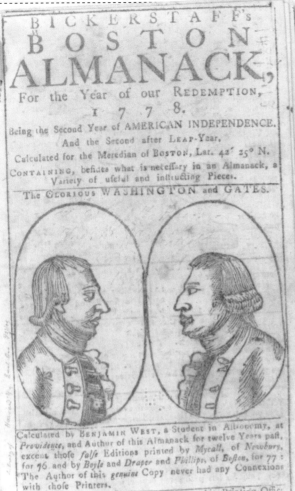

BICKERSTAFF's
BOSTON
ALMANACK,
For the Year of our REDEMPTION,
1778.
Being the Second Year of AMERICAN INDEPENDENCE.
And the Second after LEAP-YEAR.
Calculated for the Meridian of BOSTON, Lat. 42° 25° N.
CONTAINING, besides what is necessary in an Almanack, a
Variety of useful and instructing Pieces.
The GLORIOUS WASHINGTON and GATES.

Calculated by BENJAMIN WEST, a Student in Astronomy, at
Providence, and Author of this Almanack for twelve Years past,
except those false Editions printed by Mycall, of Newbury,
for 76 and by Boyle and Draper and Phillips, of Boston, for 77:
The Author of this genuine Copy never had any Connexions
with those Printers.
DANVERS: Printed by E. RUSSELL, at his Printing-Office,
late the Bell-Tavern. (Pr. 12/. per Dozen and 1/. 6d. single.)

◀ *The portraits of Washington and Gates are not very heroic, as was common at the time: that might suggest they are quite realistic.*

## AS THEY SAW IT

"The fatigue in that advanced redoubt was so great for want of sleep, that many faces were so swelled they could scarcely see out of their eyes... They were constantly on the lookout for the shells that were continually falling among them. It was by far the most dangerous post on the lines."

—Colonel William Moultrie describes Charleston's defenses during the siege.

## SOURCE EXPLORED

*Bickerstaff's Boston Almanack* was an annual publication full of useful dates and astronomical information, such as the time of sunrise and sunset throughout the year. This edition was published in 1778, "The Year of Our Redemption." The front cover has two portraits showing George Washington (left) and Horatio Gates. The drawings are not very flattering, which might mean they are quite realistic. The heroic status of the Patriot commanders reflected a growing confidence among Americans in general. Even after the defeats in South Carolina in 1780, morale in the Continental Army remained high. The Americans were also boosted by international support from France and, later, Spain. In October 1780 they won a victory at King's Mountain in South Carolina—the balance was again tipping in the Americans' favor.

# LAST BATTLES

American victories at King's Mountain (October 7, 1780) and the Cowpens (January 17, 1781) helped stop the British advance in the South. The Battle of Guilford Courthouse in March 1781 was a British victory, but it came at such a high cost that it weakened General Charles Cornwallis's forces. In early September, Cornwallis won another costly victory at the Battle of Eutaw Springs. The colonial troops led by General Nathanael Greene were weakening the British forces.

▲ This nineteenth-century image shows Molly Pitcher taking over her husband's cannon after he was wounded in action.

BATTLE OF GUILDFORD,

Fought on the 15th of March 1781.

One English Mile.

A. The Advance of Part of the Continentals who broke the British Center, and afterwards fell back to their original position.

British
Americans

Court House

Third & Last Position

Second Position after the Americans Road the Retreat

ORDER OF BATTLE

## SOURCE EXPLORED

This contemporary map records the battle at Guilford Courthouse on March 15, 1781. Cornwallis threw his men straight into battle after a twelve-hour march. They drove away two lines of American militia, but a third line formed by the Continental Army withdrew in a fighting retreat. It was a great victory for Cornwallis, but he had lost yet more men and it had not been a decisive victory.

◀ *The map of Guilford Courthouse shows the positions of the two sides and the direction of the American retreat.*

American morale was boosted by stories such as that of Molly Pitcher. At the Battle of Monmouth in 1778, Mary Hays carried pitchers of water for the soldiers, earning her nickname.

66 One little incident happened during the heat of the cannonade, which I was eye-witness to, and which I think would be unpardonable not to mention. A woman whose husband belonged to the Artillery, attended with her husband at the piece [cannon] the whole time. While in the act of reaching [for] a cartridge and having one of her feet as far before the other as she could step, a cannon shot from the enemy passed directly between her legs without doing any other damage than carrying away all the lower part of her petticoat. Looking at it with apparent unconcern, she observed that it was lucky that it did not pass a little higher... and continued her occupation. 99

# BATTLE FOR YORKTOWN

▲ *This map of the siege was drawn in France in 1781; it shows the lines of French ships blockading Chesapeake Bay.*

In summer 1781 George Washington heard that a French fleet was sailing to Chesapeake Bay. Nathanael Greene had trapped Cornwallis at Yorktown. Washington headed south, where the French warships blockaded the British position. Some 17,000 Americans and French surrounded 8,300 British and Germans. The Americans now had heavy guns and more cannons than the British. Cornwallis could not hope for reinforcements.

## SOURCE EXPLORED

A French artist drew this engraving in about 1781 showing the British troops at Yorktown. It was colored later. The British are trapped between the Continental Army on land and the ships of the French navy on the York River. Yorktown is in the background. The numbers of ships and American soldiers are exaggerated, but they help show how hopeless the British position was. Cornwallis was heavily outnumbered. After weeks of bombardment—Yorktown was virtually destroyed by fire caused by artillery shells—with supplies running low, he learned that reinforcements from New York were delayed.

## AS THEY SAW IT

❝ We were on duty in the trenches twenty-four hours, and forty-eight hours in camp... The greatest inconvenience was the want of good water, there being none near our camp but nasty frog ponds where all the horses in the neighborhood were watered, and we had to wade through the skirts of the ponds to get at water in any wise fit for use. ❞

—Joseph Plumb Martin of the Continental Army describes life during the siege of the British positions at Yorktown.

◀ In this image, confused British horsemen are trapped between enemies on land and at sea.

# THE BRITISH SURRENDER

The siege at Yorktown lasted twenty-one days. The American cannon fire was extremely accurate, and British resistance weakened under the bombardment. With no possibility of extra supplies or troops arriving, General Charles Cornwallis had no choice. He surrendered on October 19, 1781. British reinforcements arrived five days later, but the war was over. The United States had won its independence.

▼ Cornwallis' deputy tries to surrender his sword to Washington, who instead points him toward his own deputy.

York. Virginia 17.th Octr. 1781

Sir

I propose a Cessation of Hostilities for Twenty four hours, and that two Officers may be appointed by each side to meet at Mr. Moore's house to settle terms for the surrender of the posts of York & Gloucester. I have the honour to be

Sir

Your most obedient & most humble Servant

Cornwallis

His Excellency General Washington &c. &c. &c.

◀ Cornwallis wrote politely to Washington, but then did not attend the surrender himself, as etiquette would require.

## SOURCE EXPLORED

Cornwallis sent this note to George Washington on October 17, 1781. He proposes a ceasefire so that talks can be held about a surrender. Washington refused the British request to surrender with military honor. This was because he believed the British had acted dishonorably during the conflict.

General Charles Cornwallis writes to his superior, Sir Henry Clinton, on October 19, 1781, from Yorktown, Virginia.

66 It would have been wanton [shameful] and inhuman to the last degree to sacrifice the lives of this small body of gallant soldiers, who had ever behaved with so much fidelity and courage, by exposing them to an assault which... could not fail to succeed. I therefore proposed to capitulate; and I have the honour to enclose to your Excellency the copy of the correspondence between General Washington and me on that subject, and the terms of capitulation agreed upon. I sincerely lament that better could not be obtained, but I have neglected nothing in my power to alleviate the misfortune and distress of both officers and soldiers. 99

# WASHINGTON'S TRIUMPH

▲ *This print from the 1860s shows Washington and his generals arriving in New York City in November 1783.*

After his victory at Yorktown, Washington resigned his commission. In 1783, the Treaty of Paris with Britain confirmed American independence. Washington and other Americans debated the nature of a federal government. A new Constitution was approved in 1787. In 1789, George Washington became the first president of the United States.

## SOURCE EXPLORED

A French engraver created this portrait of George Washington in the 1780s to celebrate the American victory. Washington wears his military uniform. He stands outside his campaign tent while a servant looks after his horse. In his hands he holds copies of the American treaty of alliance with France and the Declaration of Independence. The torn papers by his feet are attempts at reconciliation from Britain. The French were determined to make sure that Britain would not be on good terms with the Americans. That would help weaken Britain's global power.

▲ The portrait of Washington was intended to underline the close links between the new United States and France.

## TREATY OF PARIS

Signed on September 3, 1783, the Treaty of Paris acknowledged America's independence from England and formally ended the Revolutionary War. John Adams, Benjamin Franklin, Henry Laurens, and John Jay negotiated and signed the treaty. The treaty established the boundaries of the United States and British North America. It also encouraged the thirteen new states to pay British subjects back for any confiscated property.

# TIMELINE

| | |
|---|---|
| **1763** | *The Treaty of Paris ends the French and Indian War. The Proclamation of 1763 limits colonial settlement and angers Americans.* |
| **1764** | *The British introduce a sugar tax.* |
| **1765** | ***March:** The British impose the Stamp Act.*<br>***October:** Representatives from nine colonies declare the Stamp Act unconstitutional.* |
| **1766** | ***March:** The British repeal the Stamp Act.*<br>***June:** The British impose new duties on the colonies.* |
| **1768** | *After political unrest, British troops arrive in Boston.* |
| **1770** | ***March 5:** In the Boston Massacre, British troops shoot dead five civilians.* |
| **1773** | ***December 16:** Boston Tea Party—in response to new duties on tea, Patriots throw tea from a British ship into Boston Harbor.* |
| **1774** | ***May:** The British impose the Intolerable Acts on Massachusetts. Americans react by boycotting British goods.*<br>***September:** The Continental Congress meets to coordinate opposition to the Intolerable Acts.* |
| **1775** | ***April 19:** The first shots of the war are fired at the battles of Lexington and Concord.*<br>***June 17:** The British win the first major battle of the war, at Bunker Hill.*<br>***September:** Benedict Arnold leads an American invasion of Canada.*<br>***December 31:** An American attack on Quebec is defeated and General Richard Montgomery is killed, ending the invasion of Canada.* |
| **1776** | ***March 17:** The British abandon Boston after a long siege.*<br>***July 4:** The Continental Congress issues the Declaration of Independence.*<br>***August–September:** Victories in battles at Long Island and White Plains leave the British in control of New York City.*<br>***December 26:** The Americans win a morale-boosting victory in the Battle of Trenton.* |

| | |
|---|---|
| **1777** | *January:* Washington attacks British forces an Princeton. <br> *June:* General John Burgoyne leads a British army south from Canada. <br> *October 13:* Burgoyne's army surrenders at Saratoga. <br> *September 26:* The British capture Philadelphia, forcing Congress to flee. <br> *Winter:* The Continental Army spends winter at Valley Forge, Pennsylvania, where it is constantly drilled. |
| **1778** | *February 6:* France recognizes the independent United States of America. <br> *June:* The Battle of Monmout is a hard-fought draw. |
| **1779** | *October:* The British defeat the French at Savannah, placing Georgia firmly under British control. |
| **1780** | *March–May:* The British besiege Charleston, South Carolina. <br> *August 16:* The Americans are defeated at the Battle of Camden. |
| **1781** | *January 17:* The Patriots win victory in the Battle of the Cowpens. <br> *March 15:* Cornwallis wins an expensive victory at Guilford Court House. <br> *August–October:* Cornwallis is trapped at Yorktown, Virginia. <br> *October 19:* The British surrender at Yorktown. |
| **1783** | *November 25:* The last British soldiers evacuate New York; Washington and his generals enter the city in triumph. |

# GLOSSARY

**almanac** An annual calendar that lists important dates and information such as astronomical data.

**anthem** An uplifting song associated with a particular country or cause.

**blockade** To seal off a place to prevent people or supplies entering or leaving.

**boycott** To refuse to trade with a person, organization, or country.

**colony** A settlement that is under the control of the government of another country.

**Continental Army** The army created by the Continental Congress.

**drill** Repetitive military exercises to improve soldiers' skills.

**duty** A tax charged on imports.

**engraving** A picture made by drawing an image on a sheet of metal and using it to print on paper.

**entrench** To establish a defensive position by digging trenches.

**facsimile** An exact copy of a document or image.

**Hessian** A German mercenary serving in the British Army.

**huzzah** An old word meaning to cheer.

**Loyalist** A colonial American who remained loyal to Britain.

**mercenaries** Professional soldiers who serve in a foreign army for pay.

**militia** A military force raised from the civilian population of an area.

**neutral** Not taking sides in an argument or conflict.

**Patriot** A colonial American who supported American independence.

**picket** A small group of soldiers placed as sentries.

**Redcoats** A name for members of the British Army.

**regulars** Members of a professional army.

**repeal** To overturn a law or act of Parliament.

**siege** A military operation in which an enemy position or town is cut off and forced to surrender.

**skirmish** Disorganized fighting between small groups of soldiers.

## FURTHER INFORMATION

# Books

Andrlik, Todd. *Reporting the Revolutionary War: Before It Was History, It Was News.* Naperville, IL: Sourcebooks, 2012.

Donlan, Leni. *George Washington: Revolution and the New Nation.* American History through Primary Sources. Chicago, IL: Raintree Fusion, 2006.

Micklos, John, Jr. *An Overview of the American Revolution: Through Primary Sources.* Berkeley Heights, NJ: Enslow Publishers Inc, 2013.

Parker, Christi E. *The American Revolution: Early America.* Primary Sources. Hungtington Beach, CA: Teacher Created Materials, 2008.

Samuels, Charlie. *Timeline of the Revolutionary War.* Americans at War. New York, NY: Gareth Stevens, 2011.

Wallenfeldt, Jeff. *American Revolution and the Young Republic.* Documenting America: the Primary Source documents of a nation. New York, NY: Rosen Publishing Group, 2011.

# Websites

**www.pbs.org/ktca/liberty**
Extensive website to support the PBS documentary series *Liberty!*

**www.history.com/topics/american-revolution**
History.com page with many videos about the Revolution.

**www.digitalhistory.uh.edu**
Click on "American Revolution" to access Digital History's resources for the period.

**www.historyplace.com/unitedstates/revolution**
Revolutionary War timelines on The History Place website.

**Publisher's note to educators and parents:** Our editors have carefully reviewed these websites to ensure that they are suitable for students. Many websites change frequently, however, and we cannot guarantee that a site's future contents will continue to meet our high standards of quality and educational value. Be advised that students should be closely supervised whenever they access the Internet.

## INDEX